WANDERLUST

Seattle

A Creative Guide to the City

BETSY BEIER

WEST
MARGIN
PRESS

SEATTLE

SHILSHOLE BAY

SALMON BAY

42

FREMONT

BALLARD

FISHERMEN'S TERMINAL

PUGET
SOUND

ELLIOTT BAY AND THE PUGET SOUND

SEATTLE
CENTER

ELLIOTT BAY

28

N
W E
S

PIKE PLACE MARKET

Fresh

ALKI BEACH

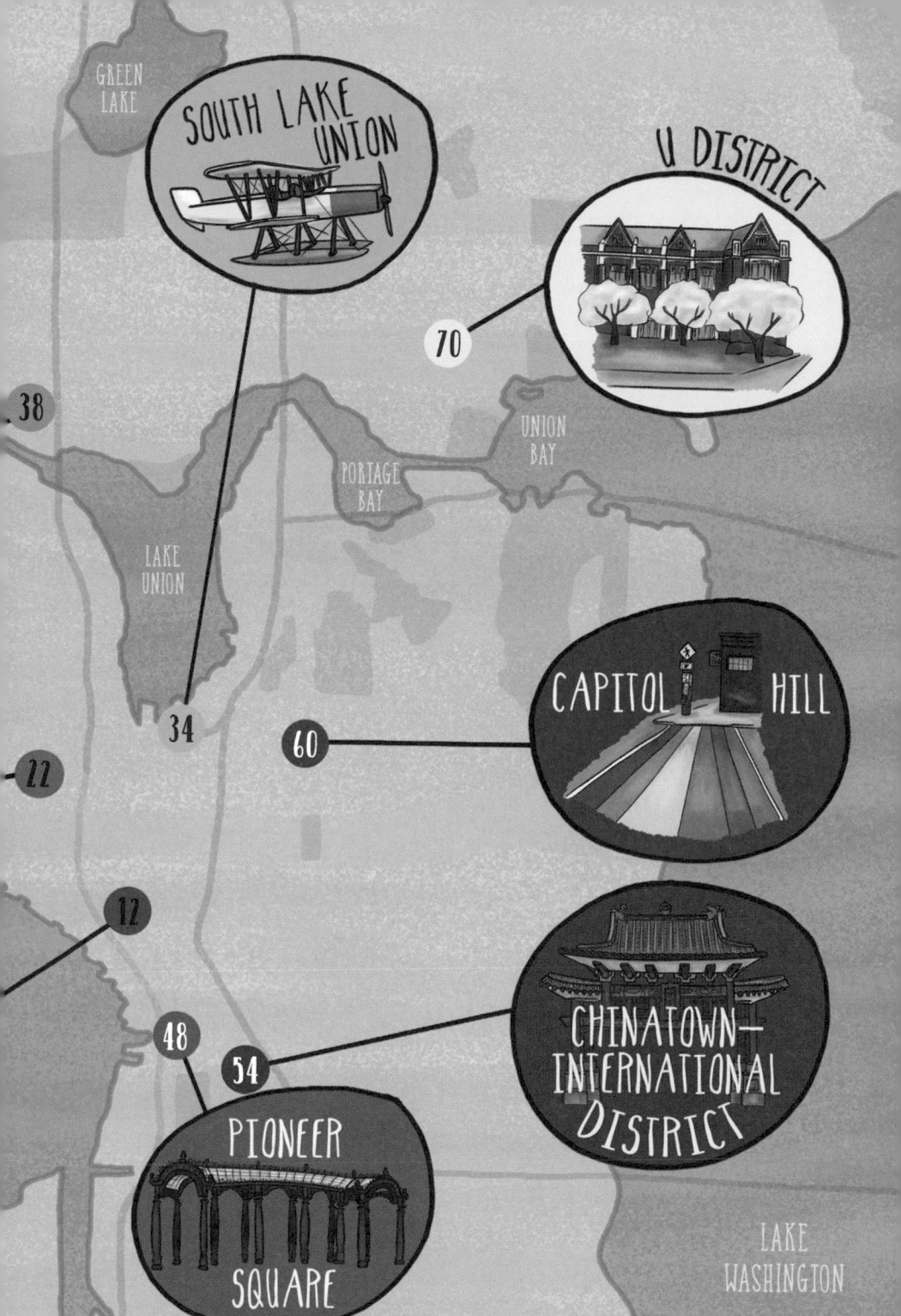

INTRODUCTION

Bound by the serene waterways of Puget Sound and the evergreen forests of the Cascade Range, Seattle is surrounded by some of the most spectacular scenery in the world. Despite its notoriously rainy climate, Seattle is made up of a culture that loves the great outdoors as much as it enjoys cozying up in a coffeehouse on a gray day. From the early days of lumber and gold to today's world of jets and high tech, Seattle continues to grow with the times yet also retains its charm by keeping its cool, down-to-earth attitude. It's no wonder so many want to experience the Seattle lifestyle!

When I travel to a new place, I love to slow down long enough to be able to capture a sliver of what life might be like to live there. Instead of seeing just the top destinations, I make time to sit at a cafe for an afternoon soaking up the vibe, or to explore a lesser-known neighborhood and watch everyday life. My idea of slowing down may be taking the time to capture the colors I see throughout the day, or to note the slang words I hear from the locals in conversation.

For me, experiential travel like this is about context, opening my eyes to learn a little about the history of the place while removing any preconceived judgement I may have brought with me. Ultimately, it's about being open to any experience that may come my way.

So join me on this creative journey as we explore the Pacific Northwest gem, Seattle!

GETTING STARTED

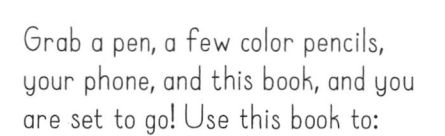

Grab a pen, a few color pencils, your phone, and this book, and you are set to go! Use this book to:

EXPLORE THE SIGHTS This book can be used as a travel guide before you head off on your journey or while you are actually at a location and looking around. Most chapters are about a specific neighborhood and some are city-wide. Within each chapter, there is some high-level history, plus interesting facts and stories to give you a taste of the area. Just use the map on page 2 to look up the destination you are interested in exploring and head out the door!

JOURNAL & SKETCH YOUR EXPERIENCE I cherish the travel journals I have kept on my trips. Some are filled with watercolor scenes of our explorations, and others are just scribbled diaries of what we did that day. For me, a travel journal is not supposed to be perfect. It's an organic document of memories and stories while in a location. There's space throughout this book to write just the facts, and room to embellish your feelings and memories of the day.

PHOTO OP
Don't miss these photo opportunities! Look for this symbol throughout the book to find nearby sights for that perfect snapshot.

GET CREATIVE This book is all about getting creative and engaging the local area you are exploring to have a unique and memorable experience. So if you have an inspiring idea, go for it! Some chapters provide artsy projects, some interactive games, while others encourage you to have fun with some creative writing. The activities are meant to be spontaneous and entertaining. But you could also save the book activities until later in the day, perhaps at a cafe, or back at the hotel as you relive your adventures.

Now, it's time to get exploring!

ART SUPPLIES

I've learned over time that for packing art supplies, fewer is always better. A few black pens, a travel watercolor set, and a couple colored pencils are typically all I need. Occasionally, I'll bring along a glue stick or tape to add a unique wrapper, ticket stub, or scrap of paper I may find to my journal. You'll find plenty of room in the diary section for all these artistic and creative endeavors and any others you can think up!

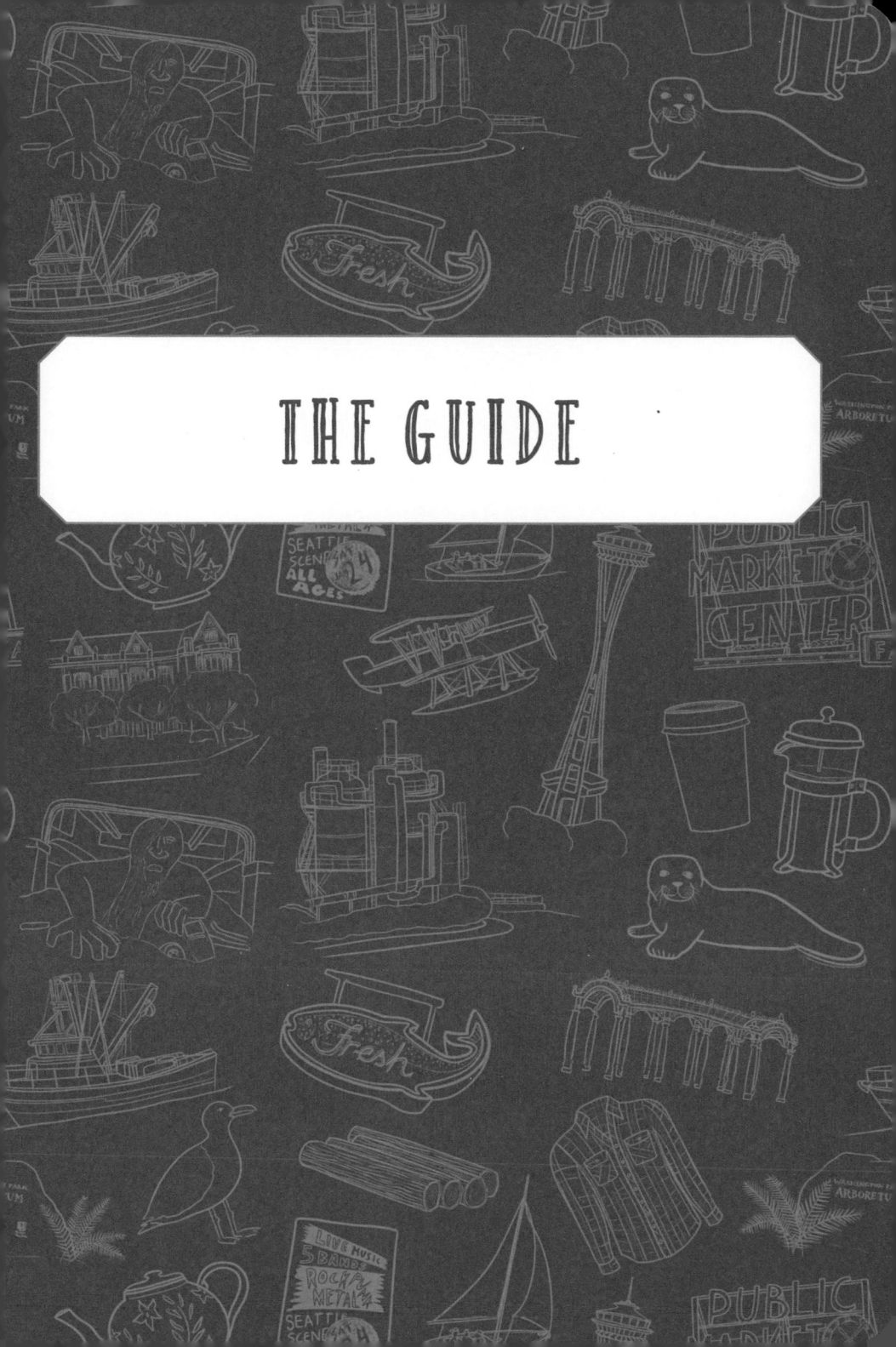

THE GUIDE

PHOTO THEMES

A photo theme is a great way to see things you may not initially notice when touring a new spot. It's like a scavenger hunt to help you see beyond the sights and uncover the patterns and unique personality of a city. All you need is your phone and a theme—a color, an object, a style, an animal, etc. As you tour the city, hunt for your theme and snap a photo when you see it. By the end of the day, you may have taken ten pictures or hundreds of them.

Once you've taken all these fabulous pictures, you can make DIY souvenir gifts for yourself! Create an art collage using a multi-photo frame, or put it all together in an artsy photo book. Here are some possible photo themes you can use.

THE SEVEN HILLS OF SEATTLE

When Seattle was being settled, many advertised it as the city of "seven hills," equating it to the other prestigious city with this moniker, Rome, Italy. Although no one can actually agree on which of the hills in Seattle make up this lucky number, Seattle is in fact made up of many more than just seven hills.

Be on the lookout for elements, vistas, or sights that capture this Seven Hills lore, whether it be a street sign indicating a grade, a store named after one of the hills, a vista from the top of one of them, or any other shot celebrating the landscape of Seattle.

THE "ORIGINAL" SEVEN HILLS

- First Hill
- Second Hill (was also Renton Hill, but now Cherry Hill)
- Yesler Hill (now Yesler Terrace)
- Denny Hill (now Denny Regrade)
- Capitol Hill
- Queen Anne Hill
- Beacon Hill
- Other notable hills: West Seattle Hill, Magnolia Bluff, Sunset Hill, Crown Hill, Mount Baker

UMBRELLAS & GRAY SKIES

Just as coffee is synonymous with Seattle, so are umbrellas and gray skies. Seattle holds the prestigious claim to being the cloudiest major city in the Lower 48 states. Although it is not the rainiest, it does get its fair share of an average of over 37 inches a year. Given these facts, umbrellas and gray skies make the perfect photo theme for your stay in Seattle. Take an hourly picture of the clouds in the sky for a couple days, and capture all the variations of gray you might see. Find a place to take pictures of umbrellas in use from above, or look for unusual umbrellas. If by chance you are in Seattle and don't experience one single rain drop or gray day, photograph the crystal-blue skies to commemorate the event!

BOATS

With lakes, canals, streams, and large bodies of water from every vista, it's almost guaranteed that during your Seattle visit you will come across a wide variety of boats. Use your camera to capture boats of a certain color, boats named after girls, or just all the boats you see. There are endless opportunities as well as boat themes to make for a great boat hunt in Seattle.

PIKE PLACE MARKET

Pike Place Market is one of the oldest continuously running markets in the US. The market first opened in 1907, when locals demanded more direct access to produce from farmers versus using a wholesaler or middleman. Less than a dozen farmers showed up on opening day, and by lunch they were all sold out. Pike Place continually grew over the decades in providing not only fresh produce but also fish, meat, baked goods, flowers, and more.

Pike Place Market began to see a downturn during WWII. More than half of the stalls became empty as the Japanese American farmers were placed in internment camps and lost their land. After the war, there was a large urban movement to the suburbs. Also, the concept of a supermarket and the plethora of refrigerators in everyone's home made a daily trip to the market unnecessary. These occurrences greatly affected the popularity and traffic to the market, and soon the aging buildings fell in disrepair.

Pike Place Market is located at Pike Street and 1st Avenue.

Multiple proposed urban renewal projects in the '60s and '70s had their eyes on Pike Place Market and were eager to redevelop the prime land into more usable spaces, such as a parking garage, high-rises, and a hotel. Fortunately, Seattleites banded together to protest these developments and urged the market be renovated to revive its purpose and celebrate its history. By the mid-1970s, this revitalization took place and the market was restored to its former glory. Now over 100 years since it first opened, Pike Place Market remains a vital part of Seattle for locals and tourists alike.

SIGNS IN THE MARKET

Pike Place Market is filled with great neon and hand-lettered signage. Snap all the pictures you can of lettering throughout the market. They will make a great photo collage when you are done!

SKETCH THE MARKET

As you meander the market, take out a few color pencils or a pen and quickly sketch the large variety of foods, produce, flowers, and crafts you see. Your loose sketches will be a great memory of the energy and pace of your market visit.

GUM WALL IN POST ALLEY

There's something truly artistic (in a disgusting sort of way) about Gum Wall in Post Alley just next to Pike Place Market. This brick wall is covered in chewing gum—lots and lots of chewing gum. At one point, prior to the wall's first cleaning in 2015, the gum in some areas was several inches thick. You may hardly even realize that over 2,300 pounds of gum were removed in the cleaning since just years later the wall filled up again. If you take too long to think about what you are looking at, you truly will want to turn and run; but before you do, take a look at the wall again and consider it as abstract art. The variety of shades of gum is quite amazing.

IS IT ART?

Explore your artsy side by taking a close-up photo of the gum wall. Add one of your favorite photo filters and see what you get. Who knows, your picture could become a work of art.

SEATTLE WATERFRONT

Seattle, like so many cities situated around bustling waterfronts, has been marred by the presence of an elevated freeway along the shores of Elliott Bay since the 1950s until recently. After four long years, "Bertha," a tunnel-boring machine, finally completed a new route such that the Alaskan Way Viaduct double-decker freeway could be removed. Even prior to the removal of the freeway, Seattle's historic waterfront had been revitalized. With ferries gliding in and out of terminals, signature seafood restaurants, the Seattle Aquarium, the Seattle Great Wheel, Olympic Sculpture Park, hotels, and more, it's obvious why this area is popular. With time, a grand promenade, a protected bike lane, seating areas, child-friendly play areas, plenty of greenery, and the spectacular views will make this one of Seattle's top neighborhoods!

WIRED SEATTLE: COFFEE CULTURE

There's no denying Seattleites love their coffee! Some say it's the weather. What better way to spend a cool, gray, drizzly day than indoors sipping a warm cup of coffee? Others claim the Scandinavian roots of many Seattleites make them inherently big coffee drinkers. Regardless of why, with a city that claims to have more shops devoted solely to coffee than any other city in the US, it's clearly a cultural phenomenon that's not going away anytime soon.

Independent coffeehouses are not a new thing either. The mid to late 1950s through the '60s sprung many bustling coffee shops, some still in existence today. Ironically, the brand which is synonymous with Seattle, Starbucks, started out as a small roastery on Western Avenue in 1971. Three coffee lovers were inspired by the worldly approach to coffee beans that Peets Coffee of Berkeley, CA, were delivering. With a nautical theme in mind, they named their shop after a character in *Moby Dick*, Starbuck. Five years later they moved to their now famous Pike Place location and the rest, as they say, is history!

Despite the hometown big-named brands, most locals patronize the independent shops. The coffeehouses are much more than just a place to get a cup of joe. They are a place to socialize, meet up with friends, and do work. Some have art galleries, and some have live music to entertain coffee drinkers. There is even a coffee shop in the Queen Anne neighborhood where an indie radio station broadcasts from!

LATTE & COFFEE CUP ART

The coffee experience in Seattle doesn't end with just a uniquely brewed cup of coffee—your coffee can also be a work of art. Many coffeehouses will serve your favorite specialty coffee with a signature design made of foamed milk on top. When you get your next decorative cup of joe, be sure to capture a photo of it. At the end of your trip you can create a collage of all the masterpieces you drank.

Another fun way to pass time in a coffee shop is to doodle on your paper cup. If you look on the internet, you will see that coffee cup art is quite amazing. Give it a try yourself and see what creations ensue!

INTERVIEW A BARISTA

Get to know one of the local baristas by conducting an interview and find out what it is like to work in a city where coffee is king!

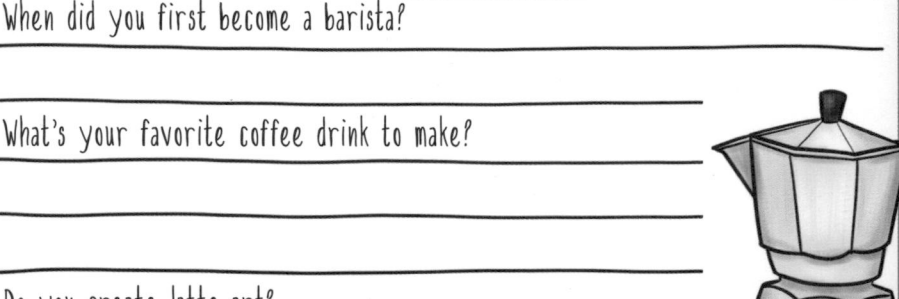

What is your name?

_____

When did you first become a barista?

_____

_____

What's your favorite coffee drink to make?

_____

_____

Do you create latte art?

_____

_____

What's the most complicated order you have gotten?

_____

_____

What's the strangest thing you've seen in your coffeehouse?

_____

_____

Why do you think Seattleites love their coffee so much?

_____

_____

Be honest: are you a coffee drinker?

_____

_____

DRAW YOUR COFFEE

Coffee is not just for drinking—it's also for art! Doodle some designs for your coffee cups, draw latte art, and let your creativity flow!

A SERIOUS BUSINESS

Drinking coffee in Seattle is much more than gulping down a cup on the go. It's quite an art form, from the worldly selection of beans and artisanal blending methods to the roasting, temperature, and filtration. Some shops offer "cupping" events, or coffee tastings, to everyday drinkers, a technical tasting process only done by professional coffee producers and buyers. There is also an emphasis on environmental practices, from ethical sourcing of beans to the distribution of used grounds for customers to feed their own gardens. Clearly Seattleites enjoy their coffee ritual.

SEATTLE CENTER

CENTURY 21 EXPOSITION

Seattle once again became the center of the world when it hosted the 1962 World's Fair, called the Century 21 Exposition in Queen Anne. The goal was to showcase science and technology of the United States in a Jet Age world. Of course, being the center of airplane and jet innovation, Seattle naturally was the perfect host.

The Fair sported futuristic designs, the most notable being Seattle's famed symbol the Space Needle. Just like all great designs, the idea of this Space Age needle was originally drawn on a placemat as an initial proposal. The rather crude drawing was taken by architect John Graham, Jr. and his team and was significantly revised into a 605-foot needle that was finally approved and built in less than a year.

SPACE NEEDLE FACTS

- Opened to the public on April 21, 1962
- Stands 605 feet high and 138 feet wide
- Named the tallest tower in Seattle from 1962 until 1969
- Offers a 43-second elevator ride, traveling 10 mph

The Space Needle is at 400 Broad Street.

GOOGIE ARCHITECTURE GALORE

Any fan of mid-century "Googie" architecture must spend time exploring Seattle Center. The Space Needle and Pacific Science Center of course take center stage with their ultra modern style, but there are many other futuristic finds in the area. Keep your camera ready, and make a game out of scouting out these Jetson-era symbols.

Other futuristic designs from the Fair that are still in use today is the Seattle Center Monorail, which took guests from Downtown Seattle to the Expo; the United States Science Pavilion, now the Pacific Science Center; the Seattle Armory, now a food pavilion; and the Washington State Coliseum, now KeyArena. Inside that Coliseum, visitors were transported via the Bubbleator, or a glass elevator, to view

The Seattle Monorail stations are at Seattle Center (on Broad Street) and Westlake Center Mall (at 5th Avenue and Pine Street).

the future at the "World of Tomorrow" exhibit. The Fair even sported a risqué area called Show Street which provided adult entertainment, including a venue called "Peep" Backstage USA. Just a small list of notable attendees to the Fair included John Glenn, Walt Disney, Bob Hope, Elvis, Prince Phillip, and Lassie. After six months and close to 10 million visitors, the Fair closed and its buildings were converted into continued usable space.

Fast forward more than 50 years and what used to be Century 21 Exposition is now the bustling Seattle Center with entertainment for all ages, including the famous and newly updated Space Needle. A trip to Seattle is not complete without visiting this lively complex.

BELGIAN WAFFLES BECOME A HIT

Of course we have to thank the Seattle World's Fair for the spectacular Space Needle and the futuristic monorail, but did you know it is also where Americans were introduced to the delicious, fluffy Belgian waffle? With his yeast batter and waffle irons from Belgium, Walter Cleyman opened two waffle stands at the Fair. America's flat pancakes were no match for the extra-large, light waffles topped with strawberries and cream. News circulated of the delicious treats and by the end of the Fair the word was out and the waffles were a fan favorite. Fun fact: The waffles were so popular, they were even featured in the Elvis movie *It Happened at the World's Fair.*

The Pacific Science Center is at 200 2nd Avenue North.

THINGS TO SEE IN SEATTLE CENTER

- Artists at Play
- Chihuly Garden and Glass
- Discovery Center
- International Fountain
- Museum of Pop Culture (MoPOP)
- Pacific Science Center
- Seattle Center Armory
- Seattle Children's Museum
- Seattle Repertory Theatre
- Space Needle

JET CITY AND THE BOEING BOOM

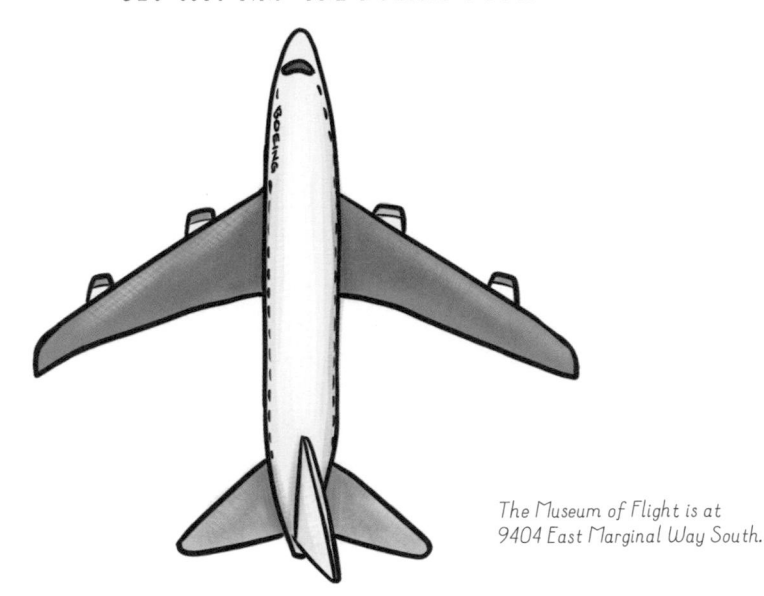

The Museum of Flight is at 9404 East Marginal Way South.

Before Seattle became the Emerald City, it was known as Jet City due to the prominence of the aerospace industry and, most importantly, the presence and success of Boeing. Boeing was first incorporated in 1916 but became a huge success during WWII when it supplied nearly 16,000 bombers within four years to the war effort. The company employed almost 50,000 people and streamlined the process of building a plane, narrowing the time from taking months to build one plane to building over 300 within the same time frame. Post-war time could have been a bust for the company, but they slimmed down employment and diversified by developing planes for the commercial airlines while still retaining its hand in military contracts. Although Seattle is no longer referred to as Jet City, Boeing's presence remains strong. As the industry continues to have its fair share of ups and downs, the Boeing saga persists.

ZIP INTO THE SPACE AGE

Just as the World's Fair brought Seattle into the future in 1962, so can you! Embellish this silhouette drawing of the Seattle skyline with Space Age additions of what the city may look like 50 years from now.

ELLIOTT BAY & THE PUGET SOUND

The Washington State Ferry system is the largest ferry system in the United States. With over 20 vessels in their fleet, the system takes commuters, local adventurers, and tourists alike to islands such as Bainbridge or Vashon, or even to a city in a different country like Victoria in British Columbia, Canada.

WASHINGTON STATE FERRIES

Seattle Ferry Terminal
at Colman Dock

To Bainbridge Island and Bremerton

Puget Sound is not only filled with ferries but is also home to spectacular wildlife, including seabirds, seals, sea lions, sea otters, porpoises, and whales (including orca and humpback) to name a few. There's no telling what you might spot on your day out on the water.

WHALE WATCHING

Puget Sound is home to many types of whales, from gray whales to humpbacks, to the iconic black-and-white orcas. Although it is possible to spot whales all year round, if you happen to be in the Seattle area from May through October, your chances increase significantly as this is when many whales are migrating the coast and salmon and other food are readily available. You can catch a ferry from Seattle to view whales, or if you prefer to stay on land, grab your binoculars and head to Alki Beach in West Seattle and see if you can spot some casually passing by.

SOUND STORIES

Hemingway led the way for this short story trend by writing just six words: "For sale: baby shoes, never worn." Now it's your turn to give it a shot in 10 words. In the spaces below, write several 10-word stories about ferries, the sea life around Seattle, or exploring Puget Sound. Try to come up with a beginning, middle, and end. If possible, even create a character!

TILLICUM VILLAGE

Instead of getting in your car to explore West Seattle and Alki Beach, the famed landing point of the settlers, take a cruise on Puget Sound to Blake Island, a Washington State Park only accessible by boat that's filled with trails, beaches, campsites, and amazing views of the Seattle skyline, Mount Rainier, and the Olympic Mountains. Along with the serene park setting, Blake Island is also home

to Tillicum Village, a cultural attraction that provides an immersive look at the Northwest Coastal Natives culture.

Birthplace of Chief Si'ahl, whom Seattle is named after, Blake Island was used as a camping site for the Suquamish tribe in the late 1780s. Once explorers discovered its location, it became a spot for logging as well a hide-out for bootleggers bringing alcohol into the US from Canada during Prohibition in the 1920s. The island continued to be occupied privately and by the US Army during the early 1900s, and by 1959 it became part of the park system.

In 1962 for the World's Fair, the historic attraction Tillicum Village was created to entertain visitors. The village quickly lost its luster

once the Fair ended, but in 2011 a large renovation put Tillicum Village back on tourists' lists. Cruise ship outings to Tillicum provide guests with a fresh salmon meal and a live performance of dancers wearing traditional costumes and masks from Washington and Alaskan coastal tribes.

ISOLATED ISLANDS BY DESIGN

Vashon Island and the San Juan Islands are the only set of islands in the Puget Sound and Salish Sea that can be accessed only by a ferry. The subject of a bridge to Vashon has been brought up many times, but the locals loudly resound with "no!" The limited access to these islands makes them a remote and truly special destination.

SKYLINE VIEW

Want to get a different perspective of Seattle? Catch a ferry to any number of places and see the Seattle skyline from the water.

SOUTH LAKE UNION

In the late 1800s the lumber industry was booming along the lake's shores as Seattle and other West Coast cities' demand grew. William Boeing, once in the lumber industry, built his first airplane (a B&W Seaplane) along the shores and conducted his first international airmail delivery to Vancouver, British Columbia, in 1919 from Lake Union.

As the lumber industry cooled and the ship canal connecting Lake Union to the Puget Sound arrived, the shipbuilding industry gained momentum around the lake with Lake Union Drydock Company being a hub. Meanwhile, industrial plants like Gas Works Park's former inhabitant Seattle Gas Light Company and Seattle City Light Lake Union Steam Plant were staples to the area.

The Lake Union Steam Plant is at 1201 Eastlake Avenue East.

AMAZON'S SPHERES

Located at 2101 7th Avenue, The Spheres contain over 40,000 species of plants. They were built to push the boundaries of an urban office by connecting workers with nature. Amazon hopes the biophilic design (a concept that supports the connecting occupants of buildings with their natural environment) will increase creativity for their employees.

Today, this area has given way to a huge tech and business boom. Not only is Amazon's headquarters in South Lake Union, but Microsoft co-founder Paul Allen's company has made large investments in developing the area with life science organizations. There is also loads of recreational fun. Ferries, sailboats, kayaks, canoes, SUPs (stand-up paddleboards), and rowboats are daily sights on the lake, even in rainy weather. For folks who love boats, the Center for Wooden Boats, an outdoor museum with historic wind-powered boats and a maritime library, is a must-visit.

The Center for Wooden Boats is at 1010 Valley Street.

Boeing's seaplane legacy can still be seen on Lake Union, as it is the busiest seaplane terminal in the country. History buffs will also enjoy the Museum of History and Industry (MOHAI) in the refurbished Naval armory building. But one of the most unique aspects of the area is the approximately 500 houseboats along the shores. This houseboat enclave (which started in the early 1900s) was once a blight for Seattleites who wanted to banish the cheap housing. By the 1960s, the houseboat lifestyle became more acceptable. Today, some of these houseboats are the most beautiful homes in Seattle.

MOHAI is at 860 Terry Avenue North.

DESIGN YOUR DREAM HOUSEBOAT

Imagine living on the water as many Seattleites do. What does your houseboat look like? Does it have a name? Don't forget to add some color to your floating home!

FREMONT

Named after two of the area's founders' hometown in Nebraska, the Fremont neighborhood of Seattle has the auspicious title "Center of the Universe." Although it's not situated in the middle of Seattle (or the middle of anything, for that matter), the neighborhood embraces this exuberant title with colorful eccentricity. The area has managed to retain its artsiness even with tech firms moving in and high-end condos popping up. For example, what other neighborhood sports an extra-large troll living under a bridge emerging from the ground holding a real VW Bug? And what about a 16-foot bronze statue of Vladimir Lenin, or a 53-foot Cold War-era rocket?

The Lenin statue is at 3526 Fremont Place North.

There is also the bold Fremont Solstice Parade, an event where crazy costumes and naked painted bodies are the norm. To top it off, the parade ends for more festivities at one of the most unique parks in the US—Gas Works Park. Rusted and cracked cylinders and old plant workings of the Seattle Gas Light Company (1906–1956) were transformed in the '70s into a public park. Sitting on the top of the hill overlooking Lake Union and Downtown Seattle, the park not only has spectacular views, but it's also the perfect spot to fly a kite.

Gas Works Park is located at 2101 North Northlake Way.

But if you still need your fix of weirdness beyond what Fremont has to offer, have no fear. Seattle does not disappoint when it comes to strange! Not only was Seattle and the surrounding area home to the fictitious vampire clan in the famous *Twilight* book (and movie) series from the mid-2000s, but the city also has a devoted voluntary group of people known as the Seafair Pirates. Yearly, these pirates make their landing at Alki Beach in early July with a full-day festival for adults and kids alike. Following their landing, they then participate throughout the summer in local festivals entertaining the crowd in their boat, the *Moby Duck*.

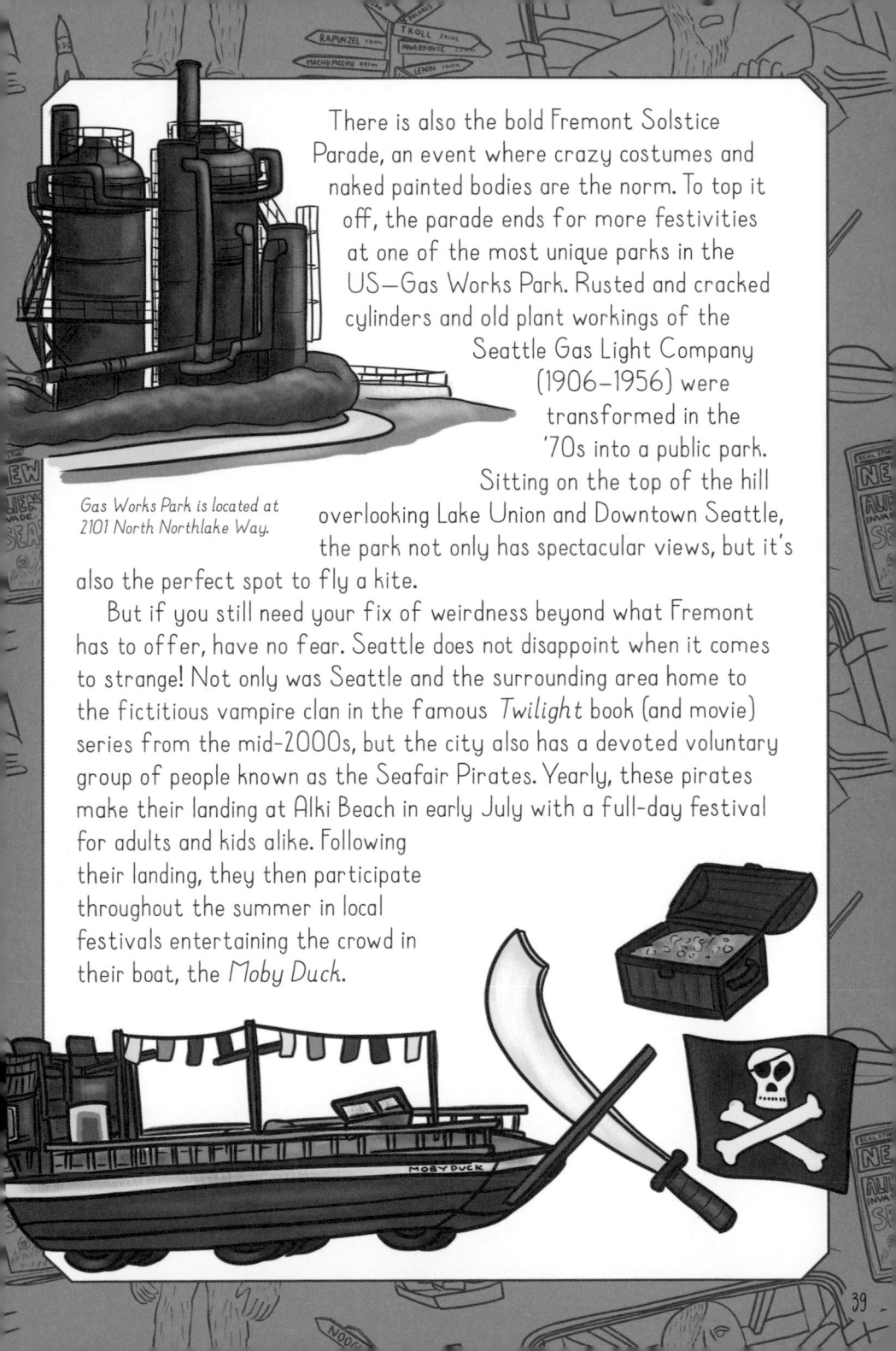

UFOS AND BIGFOOT

It's no wonder Seattle is so weird. The state of Washington holds the honor of one of the top states in the US for UFO sightings. In fact, it is reported to be the home to the first filmed evidence of a UFO as well as the 1947 Maury Island Incident, where a man reported sightings of doughnut-shaped flying saucers dumping debris on Maury Island and the Puget Sound. He also claimed to be approached by men in black the next morning, inspiration for the same named movie series some decades later.

But if UFOs aren't enough, Washington also tops the list of states with over 2,000 reports of Sasquatch or Bigfoot sightings. Many describe seeing a hairy, upright-walking, ape-like creature and hearing screams and howls. So keep your eyes peeled when out and about in Seattle. You never know what you might see!

FBI
MAURY ISLAND INCIDENT
DO NOT READ
CLASSIFIED
HIGH CLEARANCE
SECRET

REAL STORIES · REAL LIVES
NEWS
078 RAININ & GATOR
ALIENS INVADE SEATTLE

THE SEATTLE INVASION

Take turns asking your friends or travel companions to come up with words to fill in the blanks based on the part of speech or description given. Once complete, read the whole story out loud for a hilarious Seattle tale.

It was another _____ and _____ day in Seattle. I jumped off the
           [color]   [weather condition]

_____ on Westlake Ave N and popped into my favorite _____ shop to warm
[type of transportation]   [drink]

up and get my specialty latte. As I sniffed the warm _____, I looked out the window and
                                          [noun]

noticed a group of people in _____pointing at the famed Space Needle. At first
                             [name of a park]

I ignored this because it's not unusual for tourists to admire the tower, but as the crowd got

bigger, I knew something was different.

    I ran outside, looked up, and saw _____ shooting off the Space Needle Observation
                                   [noun]

Deck. Before we knew it, not one but _____ of UFOs appeared in the sky. I rubbed my eyes
                                [number]

in disbelief. These flying _____ looked identical to the top of our beloved
                        [type of transportation]

Space Needle.

    We began to hear a _____ as we watched hundreds of aliens beamed to the ground.
                        [noise]

In a panic, we all began to _____. Instinctually, it seemed we all knew where to head for
                      [verb]

protection—the Fremont Troll under the Aurora Bridge. When I arrived, it was clear I wasn't

the only one seeking protection from the _____. We huddled together and heard the
                                       [noun]

_____ noise grow and the aliens approached. We began to yell uncontrollably to overcome
[adjective]

our fear: "_____!" Bodies began to be tossed around like _____.
         [common expression]   [objects]

    I shut my eyes, fearful of what would come next. The screeching noise was soon overtaken

by loud, _____ grunts. We peered out from under the bridge and saw the most incredible
       [adjective]

sight. The Sasquatches had come to our rescue. A horde of incredibly large _____ beasts
                                          [adjective]

were fighting the aliens and winning! We cheered madly, "_____!"
                                     [exclamation]

    As the sun began to set and the aliens retreated, we gathered together to celebrate the victory

and thank the _____ of Sasquatches as they retreated back to _____ where
        [number]   [local place]

they lived. Shaken yet relieved, we realized we would make it through the night and live to see

another day. But little did we know, vampires from _____ were on their way.
                                      [local place]

The _____ on the streets from the alien invasion was too much for them to resist.
     [noun]

BALLARD

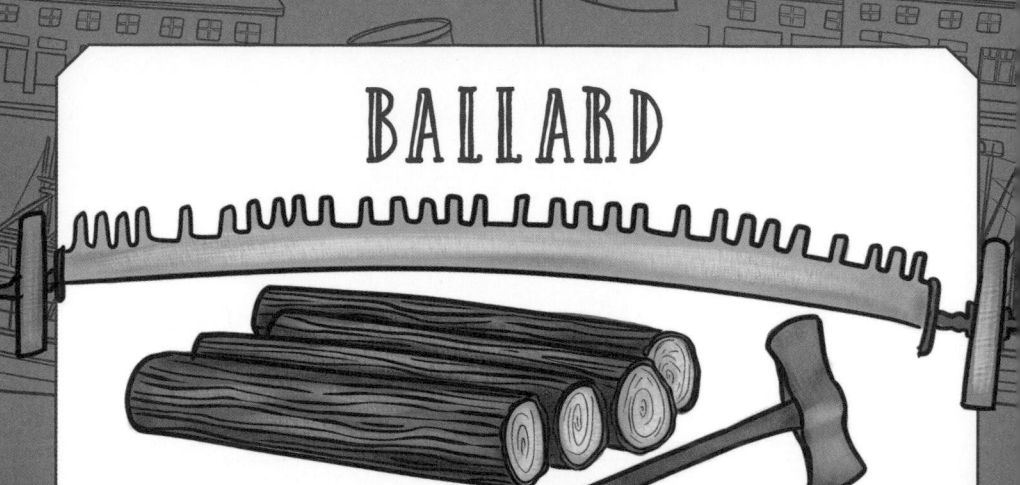

The Ballard neighborhood has always had a strong, independent identity most likely spawning from being its own city prior to being annexed to Seattle. Just as Elliott Bay and what is now Downtown Seattle were being settled, the waterfront areas of Salmon Bay were also being explored. In a lost coin toss, Captain William Rankin Ballard acquired a large acreage of the area, and the land that was seen as unworthy soon became a boon for Ballard. The mills supplying lumber and shingles to Seattle after the Great Fire in 1889 allowed this area to explode with growth. Ballard was soon nicknamed "Shingletown" and "Shingle Capital of America" as the mills cranked out more shingles than any other community nationwide.

At this same time, tumultuous events in Scandinavia led to a large influx of Norwegians and Swedish immigrants to Ballard. The climate and jobs in mills and fisheries were reminiscent of work back home and made the transition easier. Even though the city of Ballard was booming, when a lack of drinking water became an issue, it soon was annexed to Seattle in 1907.

Scandinavian heritage can still be seen throughout Ballard with Nordic-named businesses, shops, bars, and more. Ballard's sister city, Bergen, Norway, is also another nod to its heritage. Bergen shares a rainy climate, is dotted with hills, and finds influences from the fishing industry too. And just as salmon spawn in rivers in Norway and swim through the fjords to the sea, so too do salmon make their home near Ballard. The Hiram M. Chittenden Locks in the neighborhood not only transports boats of all sizes between the oceans and Puget Sound to Lake Union and Lake Washington, but they also have a 21-step fish ladder that allows salmon to return to their freshwater home and hatching grounds of Lake Washington. Today a visit to the locks and ladder is well worth it to watch the spectacle.

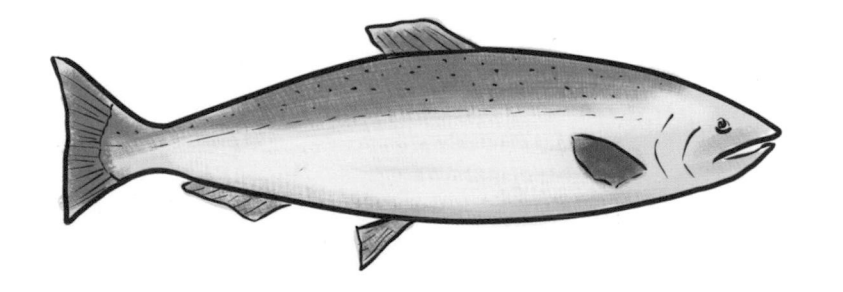

FISHERMEN'S TERMINAL

Fishermen's Terminal is at 3919 18th Avenue West.

On Salmon Bay, just east of Hiram M. Chittenden Locks, is Seattle's Fishermen's Terminal, the home of Washington's commercial fishing fleet. These fishing boats spend many months working in the open sea and off the coast of Alaska catching fish that is shipped off to buyers, restaurants, and stores all over the world. (A little over 70% of the fish caught is exported.) The work is quite dangerous, as one can see by the memorial with over 670 names honoring the deaths of fishermen while out. Some of the boats that dock at Fishermen's Terminal have also been featured on the Discovery Channel's show *Deadliest Catch*.

Wandering the docks can be an outing of its own, and if you time it right, you can buy your fresh fish for dinner right off the boats!

CATCH OF THE DAY

Fresh fish are plentiful as you wander through Fishermen's Terminal and the various stores and markets. Make sure to snap a quick pic of the catch of the day to remember your outing.

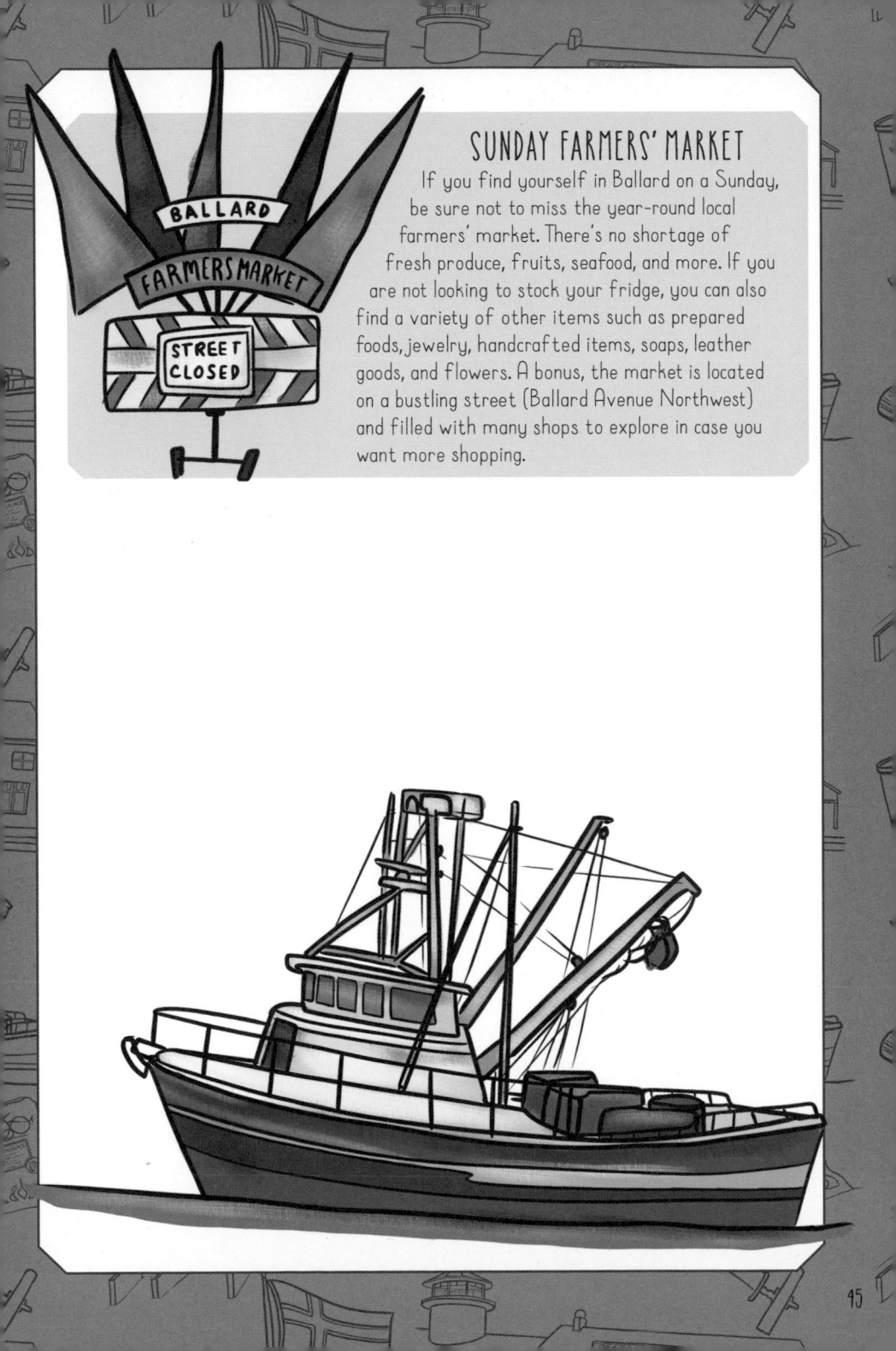

SUNDAY FARMERS' MARKET

If you find yourself in Ballard on a Sunday, be sure not to miss the year-round local farmers' market. There's no shortage of fresh produce, fruits, seafood, and more. If you are not looking to stock your fridge, you can also find a variety of other items such as prepared foods, jewelry, handcrafted items, soaps, leather goods, and flowers. A bonus, the market is located on a bustling street (Ballard Avenue Northwest) and filled with many shops to explore in case you want more shopping.

FIND INSPIRATION IN BALLARD CULTURE

In Ballard's Bergen Place Park, you can find five granite stones with etchings representing Scandinavian culture, including embroidery and weaving patterns. There is also a large mural celebrating Ballard's Scandinavian roots.

Look for hints of Ballard's Scandinavian roots in motifs, designs, and symbols of things seen while exploring the neighborhood. Now it's time to try your hand at creating a Scandinavian-inspired pattern.

Bergen Place Park is at 5420 22nd Avenue Northwest

PIONEER SQUARE

For thousands of years before white settlers arrived, the Suquamish and Duwamish Indians lived in villages surrounding what is now Pioneer Square. They called the area Zechalalitch, or the "Little Crossing-Over Place," since it was an easy route between the Duwamish River and Lake Washington. The first white settlers—approximately 24 men, women, and children led by Arthur Denny along with Carson Boren, and later joined by David "Doc" Maynard—arrived in 1851. After a few months they moved from their initial landing in West Seattle's Alki Beach to the more harbor-friendly Elliott Bay waterfront location (now Downtown and Pioneer Square). Doc set up a cabin and established a general store, The Seattle Exchange, and other settlers followed suit.

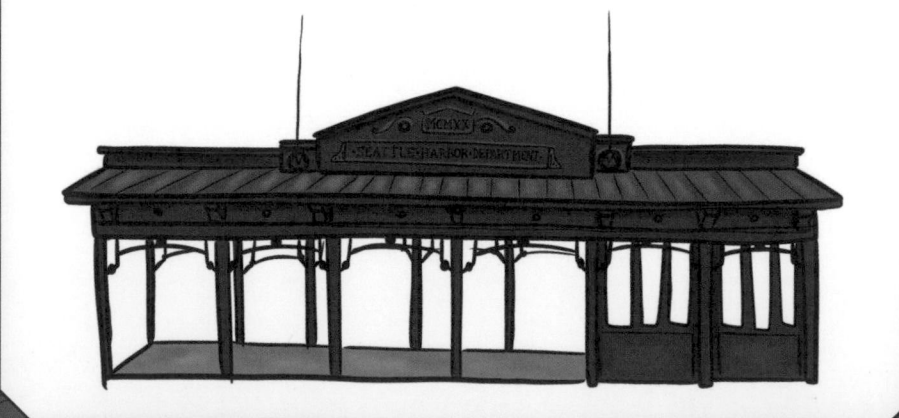

Seattle's success was cemented in 1852 when Henry Yesler decided to put a lumber mill located at the bottom of what is now Yesler Way. He set up a home nearby and built an elevated aqueduct system along the road to transport the logs from the ridges to the waterfront, creating the nickname of "Skid Road." As the village grew, the initial settlers, Denny, Boren, and Maynard, wanted to lay grounds to their claims and create a street grid for the community. It is said that this conversation didn't go as smoothly as planned, hence the triangle of strange intersections along today's Yesler Way.

Yesler Wy 200

Seattle continued to grow as San Francisco's demand for timber, coal, and other commodities stimulated business. Disaster struck in 1889 when a glue pot in a cabinet shop caught on fire and burned roughly 25 blocks within hours. Undeterred, the city rebuilt but now with brick and stone, with many of these buildings still existing today in Pioneer Square. In the process of rebuilding, the engineers decided to raise the street level one full story to fix a water drainage problem, creating catacombs of storefronts under the sidewalk level.

The Underground Tour starts at 614 1st Avenue.

In 1897, gold was discovered in the Klondike region of the Yukon, Canada; and much like San Francisco's gold rush, Seattle and Pioneer Square boomed as it became the launch point for gold diggers looking to strike it rich. Officially, the triangle that is now Pioneer Place was named and adorned with a stolen Tlingit totem pole and, a decade later, a decorative pergola to protect tourists riding the transit to the Alaska–Yukon–Pacific Exposition, Seattle's first World's Fair in 1909. Only five years later, the 484-foot-tall Smith Tower opened, the tallest building west of the Mississippi until 1962 (when the 605-foot Space Needle was completed).

Smith Tower is at 506 2nd Avenue.

CHIEF SEATTLE

HOW SEATTLE GOT ITS NAME

When the white settlers arrived, the chief of Suquamish and Duwamish Indians was Chief Si'ahl. Even when his people were being displaced from their traditional locations, Chief Si'ahl still aimed to form friendly relations with the settlers. Doc Maynard, in particular, was one whom he had formed a friendship. As the settlement initially known as Duwamps grew, Doc persuaded others to rename it to Seattle, an Anglican version of Si'ahl, in honor of the chief.

Pioneer Square soon fell on hard times for decades, starting with the Great Depression. Skid Road became filled with saloons, gambling dens, and brothels. Storefronts closed and hotels fell in disrepair. Urban renewal in the 1960s brought on some questionable urban-planning decisions, like tearing down the historic Seattle Hotel to create a parking garage (known as Sinking Ship garage). Yet, even with some wrong moves, the area slowly began to revitalize into the vibrant historic neighborhood it is today. One surprise hit was reopening the catacombs (the businesses that went underground when the street level was raised) as a tourist attraction. Today you can still see the totem pole (a second version) and the decorative pergola (reconstructed after an accident) at Pioneer Place much like it looked at the turn of the twentieth century!

The Sinking Ship garage is at 2nd Avenue and Yesler Way.

THREE GUYS WALK INTO A BAR

It's the mid-1800s and Arthur Denny, Doc Maynard, and Henry Yesler are sitting at a bar in Pioneer Square having a heated conversation about how to lay out Seattle's street grid. Write the dialogue below.

"Do you like Doc Way or Maynard Avenue?"

"Enough with the saloons, what this town needs is a good cup of coffee!"

CHINATOWN — INTERNATIONAL DISTRICT

Chinese, Japanese, and Southeast Asian immigrants have played a vital role in the development of Seattle, even after being faced with numerous challenges and controversial treatment. Only 10 years after Denny's crew settled in Elliott Bay, the first Chinese immigrant Chun Ching Hock arrived in 1860. From the 1870s to 1880s, the Seattle Chinese population grew significantly, with residents working as cooks, laundrymen, and servants as well as hard laborers (in lumber mills, coal mines, railroads, and industries) helping to build the booming city. Racism was rampant, and many times the Chinese were literally kicked out of town, but in time the Chinese population rebounded as people returned to continue to support the growth and prosperity of the city. The tight-knit community stayed together despite numerous regrades of hillsides to form Seattle's Chinatown area.

Meanwhile, toward the end of the nineteenth century, the Japanese population also grew in Seattle as Japanese immigrants came to work in the railroads, logging, and cannery industries. By 1920 the Japanese population had grown to roughly 8,000 people living adjacent to Chinatown in a neighborhood called Nihonmachi, or Japantown. Sadly, the internment order of Japanese Americans in 1942 took a huge toll on the community. Following the war, many Japanese decided not to return to what they knew as home in Japantown, Seattle.

Along with Chinatown and Japantown, Seattle has also seen a large influx of Southeast Asian cultures. In the 1930s the Filipino community was thriving with some 1,600 residents. By the '70s, the Vietnamese community grew, forming Little Saigon, adjacent to Chinatown and Japantown. Other Southeast Asian immigrants such as Cambodians and Laotians followed. Today, these three cultural areas of Chinatown, Japantown, and Little Saigon have been renamed Chinatown–International District.

SEE THE HISTORIC CHINATOWN GATE

The ornate and colorful Chinese gate is a recent addition to the neighborhood. Like other Chinatown districts in cities like San Francisco and Los Angeles, the Seattle community wanted a formal gate to announce the entrance to the neighborhood. The Gate is said to bring good luck and strength to the community as well as create a clear visual indicator of this must-see neighborhood.

Hing Hay Park is at 423 Maynard Avenue South.

Walking through this neighborhood is like taking a trip to various Asian countries. There are many stores, restaurants, parks, museums, and hotels to visit. At Hing Hay Park you will find an ornate pagoda (from Taiwan) and locals relaxing, playing chess, or practicing Tai Chi. Nearby, Uwajimaya, a Japanese grocery store, has become a full-fledged tourist attraction because of not only the items it carries but also the history. Likewise, the artsy store Kobo at Higo occupies the location of the historic Higo 10 Cent Store (which became Higo Variety Store). The story of the business run by the Murakami family for over 75 years has been preserved with displays honoring the long history. But a visit to Wing Luke Museum of the Asian Pacific American Experience, with its numerous exhibits touting the 150-year history of Asian & Pacific Islanders in Seattle, is the perfect way to sum up the impact these cultures have had on this city.

The Higo Variety Store is at 602-608 South Jackson Street

ALLEYS OF CHINATOWN—INTERNATIONAL DISTRICT

Alleyways like Canton, Maynard, and Nihonmachi historically played a vital part of what life was like living in this neighborhood. Businesses and community life used to be thriving in

these alleyways, but in more recent times the alleys became unwalkable with dumpsters and trash from neighboring businesses. Several different community efforts in the past few years attempted to reclaim these alleyways to their former importance to the community.

From the removal of the dumpsters to the addition of art installations, outdoor seating, and refurbished storefronts, the neighborhood has taken back what was once an eyesore to create revitalized gathering areas for the community to enjoy.

JAZZ ON JACKSON STREET

From the early 1900s through WWII, many African Americans migrated to Seattle for job opportunities. With them they brought vibrant musical styles of jazz, swing, and rhythm and blues that had originated in the Midwest and South and eventually developed a congregation of over 30 nightclubs on Jackson Street, where the music was celebrated. Many musicians who played in these locations went on to international fame, including Quincy Jones, Ray Charles (originally from Florida), and Jimi Hendrix.

TRAVEL ABROAD WITHOUT A PASSPORT!

Sketch signs, packaging, and tchotchkes unique to this district to commemorate your visit.

CAPITOL HILL

The Moore Mansion is at 811 14th Avenue East.

Capitol Hill neighborhood gets its name from developer James A. Moore, who bought one of the last undeveloped plots of land in the late 1800s–early 1900s. It is said that Moore wanted to lure Washington's state capital from Olympia to Seattle, hence the name. Others claim he named it after the neighborhood his wife had lived in Denver. Regardless of Capitol Hill's naming origin, Moore transformed the land with sidewalks, streets, and sewers to create a neighborhood targeted to the wealthy. Today, just south of Volunteer Park along 14th Avenue East is one of Seattle's wealthiest areas known as Millionaire's Row.

Volunteer Park Conservatory is at 1400 East Galer Street.

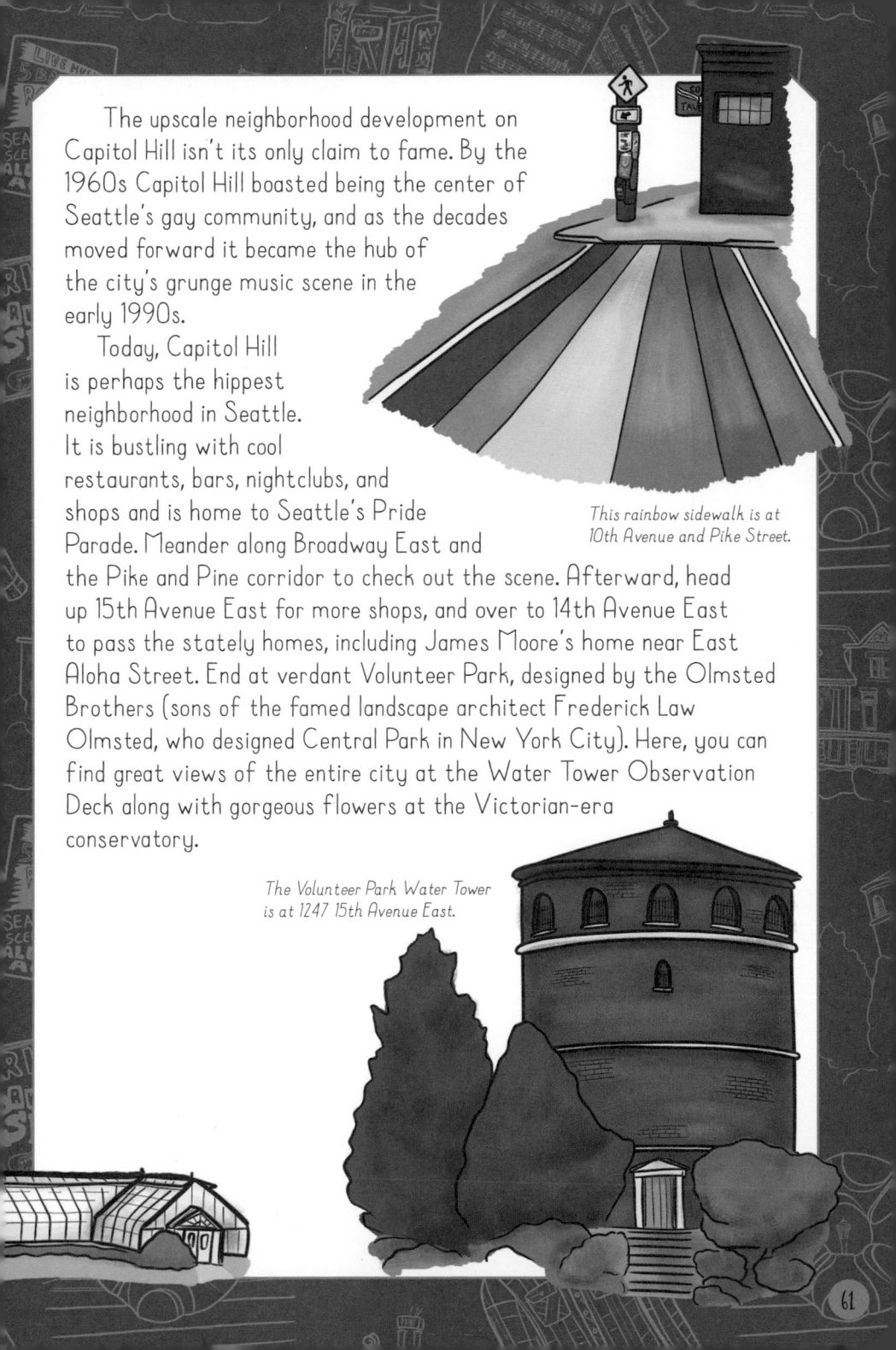

The upscale neighborhood development on Capitol Hill isn't its only claim to fame. By the 1960s Capitol Hill boasted being the center of Seattle's gay community, and as the decades moved forward it became the hub of the city's grunge music scene in the early 1990s.

Today, Capitol Hill is perhaps the hippest neighborhood in Seattle. It is bustling with cool restaurants, bars, nightclubs, and shops and is home to Seattle's Pride Parade. Meander along Broadway East and

This rainbow sidewalk is at 10th Avenue and Pike Street.

the Pike and Pine corridor to check out the scene. Afterward, head up 15th Avenue East for more shops, and over to 14th Avenue East to pass the stately homes, including James Moore's home near East Aloha Street. End at verdant Volunteer Park, designed by the Olmsted Brothers (sons of the famed landscape architect Frederick Law Olmsted, who designed Central Park in New York City). Here, you can find great views of the entire city at the Water Tower Observation Deck along with gorgeous flowers at the Victorian-era conservatory.

The Volunteer Park Water Tower is at 1247 15th Avenue East.

SEATTLE GRUNGE

Counterculture was not new to Seattle when grunge music began to play. Feeding from its West Coast neighbor San Francisco, the hippie culture in Seattle as well as the gay community were thriving before the first grunge chords were strum. This acceptance of counterculture and nonconformist ideals helped propel the early grunge bands forward in creating an alternative sound that was not mainstream.

In the early and mid-'80s, some bands around Seattle began mixing heavy metal and punk music to form a new kind of "scummy" or "dirty" sound. As the sounds grew in popularity, so did the number of bands in the area that played this new vibe. Soon, people began to refer to their grimy sound as "grunge." Grunge bands played in venues across the city such as The Crocodile, The Showbox, and The Off Ramp (now El Corazón). A small recording label called Sub Pop Records was formed and signed the now famous bands Nirvana, Soundgarden, and Mudhoney.

Grunge music touted traditional rock and roll power chords but also added more dissonant or minor tunings. Along with the heavy metal guitar riffs, distortion, and angst-ridden lyrics, the new genre became a hit. By the early '90s, grunge music topped the Billboard charts and in turn grew beyond just music to influence fashion trends and more. What started as an alternative counterculture movement soon became the definition of Seattle culture and the greater Pacific Northwest.

FIND A MURAL
Capitol Hill is bursting with colorful murals that make the perfect backdrop for an artsy photo.

FAMOUS MUSICIANS & BANDS FROM THE CITY

Although Seattle has become synonymous with grunge music, the city has had a vibrant music scene for decades. That's why there's a whole museum dedicated to the music scene and culture—MoPOP, or the Museum of Pop Culture. There was a lively jazz scene in the city in the 1940s, and the psychedelic rock of Jimi Hendrix in the late '60s. There was even the smooth sounds of Kenny G in the '80s. Below is a list of just some of the popular musicians and bands from Seattle.

Jimi Hendrix
Nirvana
Pearl Jam
Soundgarden
Chris Cornell
Alice in Chains
Mudhoney
Temple of the Dog

Foo Fighters
Candlebox
Heart
The Presidents of the United States of America
Nevermore
Sir Mix-a-lot
Kenny G

The Museum of Pop Culture is located at 325 5th Avenue North.

SING YOUR HEART OUT

The lyrics to many grunge songs can be quite poetic but often also brooding, filled with angst and self doubt. The stories they tell are personal, emotional, and filled with meaning, but may appear a bit confusing until they are read more deeply. Write a grunge song about your time in Seattle or exploring Capitol Hill.

"BLACK HOLE SUN"

One of the most famous songs by Seattle band Soundgarden is called "Black Hole Sun." It is apparently named after a sculpture by Isamu Noguchi in Capitol Hill's Volunteer Park that is aptly named *Black Sun*. The sculpture is shaped like a doughnut with a hole in the middle that when peered through frames the famed Space Needle.

The band not only used this sight in their music, but it's also been noted that their name stems from an outdoor public art works called *A Sound Garden* on the National Oceanic and Atmospheric Administration campus in north Seattle. The artwork by Douglas R. Hollis is made up of giant structures that whistle and howl when it is windy.

PARKS OF SEATTLE

It's no wonder the nickname of Seattle is the Emerald City. Not only do forests of evergreen trees line the highways, but head to any one of the many parks and you will agree that there is no shortage of the color green! Seattleites have always placed great value on their parklands. When the Olmsted brothers were hired in the early 1900s to develop a park plan for the city, they encouraged the citizens to embrace their hilltops and waterfronts and adorn them with parks. The city obliged and incurred a large tax rate to acquire the appropriate lands. Over 100 years later, their commitment to these public spaces throughout the years shows in the breadth and imagination of each park.

From the meadowlands, forests, streams, and sand dunes overlooking Puget Sound at the 534-acre Discovery Park, to the hills, waterfalls, ponds, bridges, and Kubota Garden, the traditional Japanese garden in the southern portion of the city, Seattle has numerous parks to explore. But what makes Seattle's parks stand out is how they have employed creative ways to reuse past urban or industrial blights and make them into something usable and beautiful.

For instance, Gas Works Park embraced its gas plant roots to form a stunning park. When a freeway came to town, Seattle again decided to create a unique outdoor space called Freeway Park. This recreation area is above I-5 and has walls, stairs, and fountains that give way to views of the cars. Another example is Olympic Sculpture Park owned by the Seattle Art Museum. Capitalizing on the spectacular waterfront, this park was created on an old industrial site and even includes active freight railroad tracks.

But if you are wanting to see one of Seattle's oldest parks, an afternoon at Washington Park Arboretum should be on your list. In spring, Azalea Way puts on quite a show when azaleas and the cherry trees are in full bloom.

Freeway Park is at 700 Seneca Street.

There are several different winding trails that will lead you past the wide collection of trees (oaks, conifers, maples, mountain ashes, magnolias, and more). Also, in the southern part of the park is the Seattle Japanese Garden, a destination on its own. So pack a picnic lunch and head to these urban oases to understand why Seattle is the Emerald City.

NATURE WALK

Take a nature walk in one of Seattle's parks and use the prompts below to experience the beauty around you.

Color this square to capture the color palette of your walk.

Whether it's birds along the wetlands or bugs amongst the trees, make a quick sketch of the animals you see on your walk.

Make a collage with fallen leaves.

Doodle shapes of the different leaves you see.

Walk along the waterfront at Foster and Marsh Islands and capture the waterlilies and canoers.

Create a portrait of a mushroom.

Relax at a bench or gazebo and sketch your view.

UNIVERSITY DISTRICT

the AVE

The University District, or U District, is aptly named because the neighborhood is dominated by the largest college in the state, University of Washington (UW). The University initially was located in Downtown Seattle, but in the mid-1890s it moved to its current location. Before the University arrived, the area was called Brooklyn, like the borough in New York City, because it, too, was located across the water from the larger part of the city.

Once the University settled in and the area was annexed to Seattle, the main goal was to get efficient transportation across Lake Union to connect the neighborhood. The street trolley's arrival to University Station on University Way helped build the area further, but it wasn't until the announcement that the University of Washington campus would host the Alaska–Yukon–Pacific Exposition (known as A-Y-P) in the summer of 1909 that the neighborhood, the University and University Way (known as The Ave), truly blossomed.

Drumheller Fountain is at the north end of Rainier Vista.

SIGHTS ON CAMPUS

At the time, there were only three buildings that made up the campus, so the opportunity was a coup for formally establishing UW. The Olmsted brothers (who were already involved in park planning in the city) were selected and began designing the layout. The chosen main focus of the exposition was Mount Rainier with a pool and small waterfalls forming the central axis that let into a circular pool called the Geyser Basin. This corridor was named Rainier Vista and is still the prominent layout of UW today, with Drumheller Fountain being where the Geyser Basin once was. A few buildings, like Architecture Hall and Cunningham Hall, also remain and are wonderful legacies of the A-Y-P.

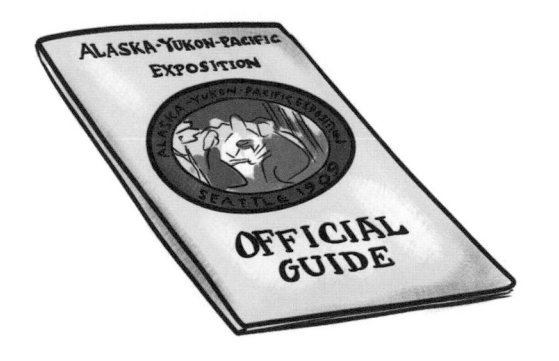

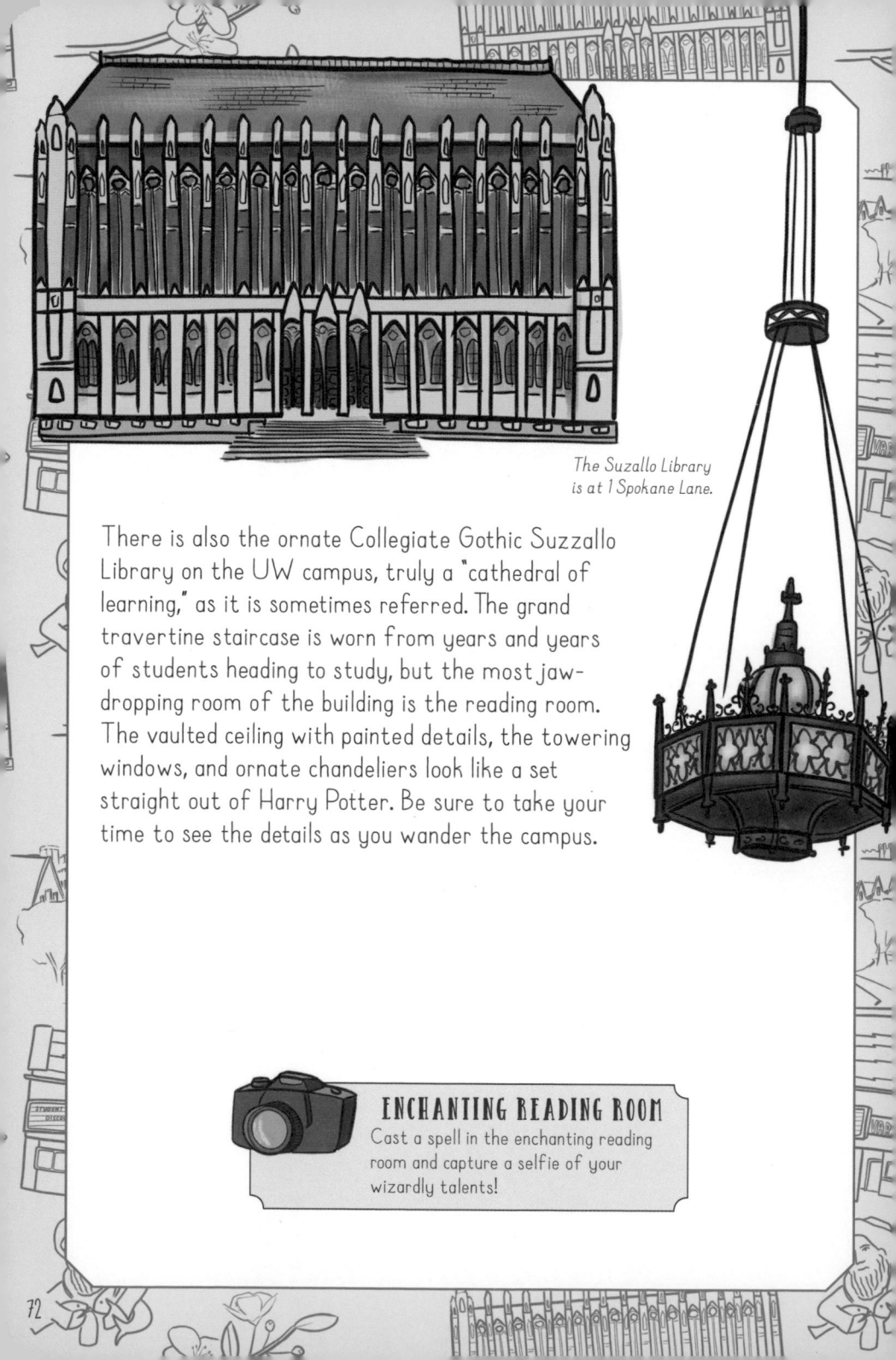

The Suzallo Library is at 1 Spokane Lane.

There is also the ornate Collegiate Gothic Suzzallo Library on the UW campus, truly a "cathedral of learning," as it is sometimes referred. The grand travertine staircase is worn from years and years of students heading to study, but the most jaw-dropping room of the building is the reading room. The vaulted ceiling with painted details, the towering windows, and ornate chandeliers look like a set straight out of Harry Potter. Be sure to take your time to see the details as you wander the campus.

ENCHANTING READING ROOM
Cast a spell in the enchanting reading room and capture a selfie of your wizardly talents!

CHERRY BLOSSOMS IN THE QUAD

One of the most closely tracked events that happens at UW each year is the blooming of the cherry blossoms in the Quad. There are almost 30 cherry trees that line the rectangular walkways surrounded by regal Collegiate Gothic-style buildings. Websites track the weeks (and days) at which the cherry blossoms will be in full bloom.

DRAW SOME GROTESQUES

Adorning the Collegiate Gothic architecture on campus are over 100 sculptures decorating the eaves and buildings known as grotesques. They closely resemble gargoyles, but the difference is they do not spout water. The grotesques on Suzzallo Library are of 18 historic people who symbolize learning and culture. Other grotesques on campus are characters that are a commentary on the context of the world at the time. For instance, there is a gas-masked soldier reminiscent of wartime on one building, and a women doing domestic chores representing home economics on another. Draw your own grotesques to this building that reflect characters in today's world.

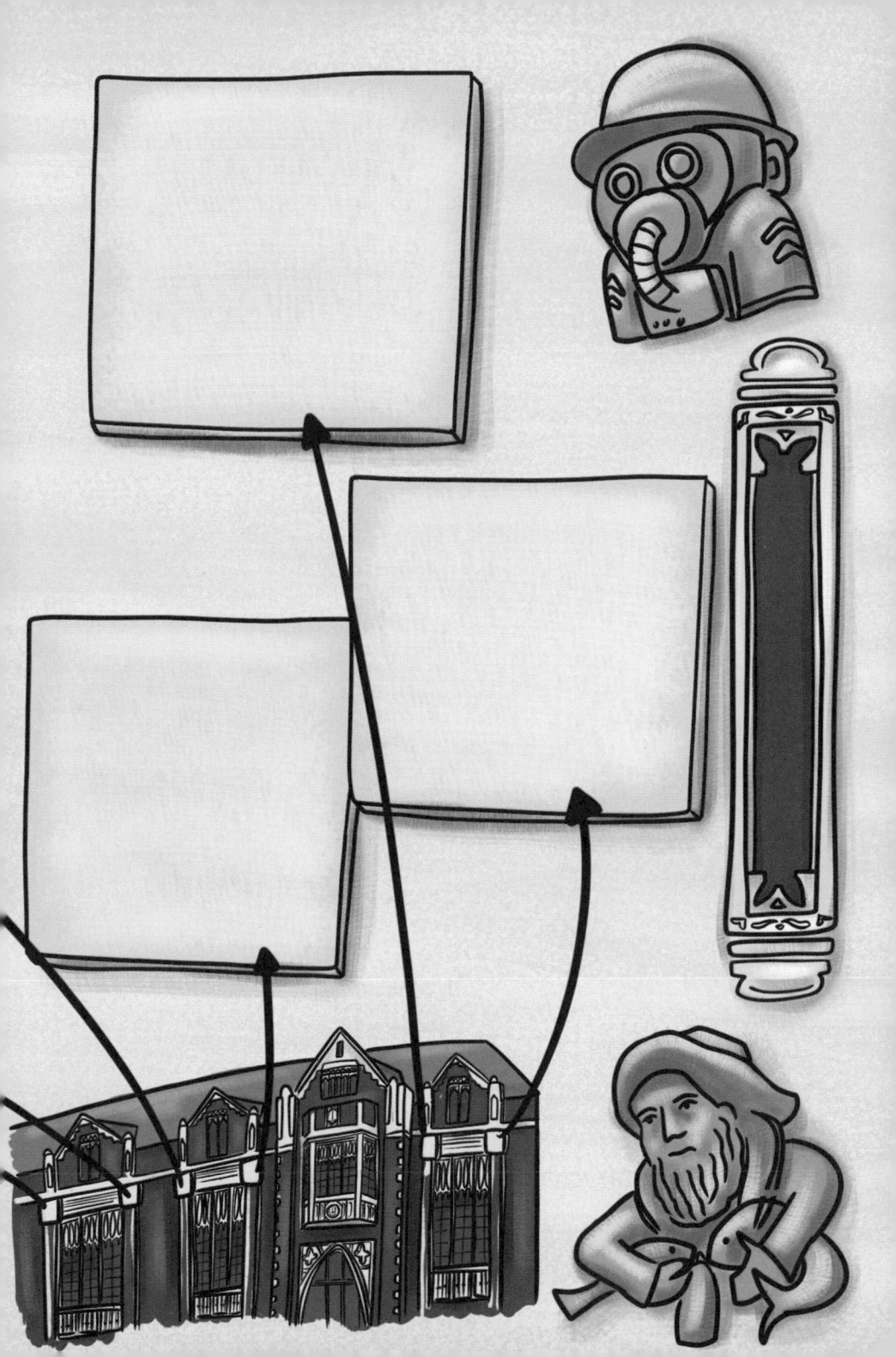

I SPY SEATTLE

As you tour around Seattle, be sure to check off seeing the uniquely Seattle sights listed here:

☐ *Eagle* by Alexander Calder (Olympic Sculpture Park, Waterfront)

☐ Bronze dance steps (on Broadway in Capitol Hill)

☐ Walrus decoration (on Arctic Club Building, 700 3rd Avenue, Pioneer Square)

☐ Pinball games (Pinball Museum, 508 Maynard Avenue South, International District)

☐ *Hammering Man* by Jonathan Borofsky (1300 1st Avenue, in front of Seattle Art Museum downtown)

☐ Glass block sidewalks (Pioneer Square)

☐ Rachel the Pig (Pike Place Market)

☐ Totem pole (Pioneer Square)

☐ Jimi Hendrix statue (Broadway East and Pine Street, Capitol Hill)

☐ Bust of Chief Seattle (100 Yesler Way, Pioneer Square)

CHIEF SEATTLE

☐ *Waiting for the Interurban* by Richard Beyer (North 34th Street and Fremont Avenue, Fremont)

☐ A glass garden (Chihuly Garden and Glass, 305 Harrison Street, Seattle Center)

☐ *A Salish Welcome*
by Martin Oliver
(3419 Northwest 54th Street,
Ballard)

☐ *Witness Trees*
by Jennifer Dixon
(Bergen Place Park,
5420 2nd Avenue
Northwest, Ballard)

☐ Dragon on a street lamp
(Chinatown-International District)

☐ Leftover luggage
from Japanese
who were sent to
internment camps
(Panama Hotel,
605½ South
Main Street,
Chinatown-
International
District)

□ Red arch (Hing Hay Park, Chinatown–International District)

□ The Seattle Great Wheel (Pier 57-Miners Landing, Waterfront)

MINERS LANDING

EXTRA CREDIT

□ Flannel Shirt

□ Oysters

□ Jacob & Frank, the ghosts of Pike Place Market

THE JOURNAL

BEST OF SEATTLE

Fill out the lists below with your favorites from exploring Seattle.

BEST SIGHTS

BEST EATS

BEST SHOPPING

BEST DRINKS & NIGHTLIFE

BEST PARKS

_____
_____
_____
_____
_____
_____
_____
_____
_____

BEST MUSEUMS

_____
_____
_____
_____
_____
_____
_____
_____
_____

The Fremont Troll is at North 36th Street.

DAY #____

DATE _____

RATING ☆☆☆☆☆

WEATHER ☀ 🌤 ☁ ☂ 🧣

PLACES VISITED

_____
_____
_____
_____
_____
_____
_____
_____
_____

BEST EATS OF THE DAY

_____
_____
_____
_____
_____
_____
_____
_____
_____

QUOTE OF THE DAY

_____
_____
_____
_____
_____

ONLY IN SEATTLE

_____
_____
_____
_____

SOMETHING I SAW TODAY

DAY

#____

DATE _____

RATING ☆☆☆☆☆

WEATHER

PLACES VISITED

_____
_____
_____
_____
_____
_____
_____
_____
_____

BEST EATS OF THE DAY

_____
_____
_____
_____
_____
_____

🙶🙶 QUOTE OF THE DAY

_____
_____
_____
_____

ONLY IN SEATTLE

_____
_____
_____

SOMETHING I SAW TODAY

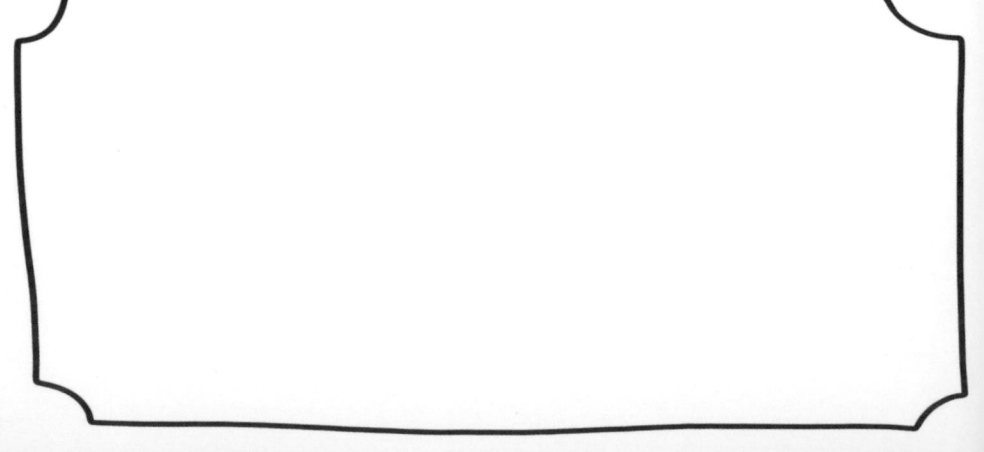

DAY

#____

DATE _____

RATING ☆☆☆☆☆

WEATHER

PLACES VISITED

_____
_____
_____
_____
_____
_____
_____

BEST EATS OF THE DAY

_____
_____
_____
_____
_____
_____

QUOTE OF THE DAY

_____
_____
_____

ONLY IN SEATTLE

ONLY HERE
ADVENTURE & FUN THINGS

_____
_____
_____

SOMETHING I SAW TODAY

DAY

#_____

DATE _____

RATING ☆☆☆☆☆

WEATHER

PLACES VISITED

_____
_____
_____
_____
_____
_____
_____
_____
_____

BEST EATS OF THE DAY

_____
_____
_____
_____
_____
_____

QUOTE OF THE DAY

_____
_____
_____
_____

 ONLY IN SEATTLE

_____
_____
_____

SOMETHING I SAW TODAY

DAY #____

DATE _____ RATING ☆☆☆☆☆

WEATHER

PLACES VISITED
_____
_____
_____
_____
_____
_____
_____
_____
_____
_____

BEST EATS OF THE DAY
_____
_____
_____
_____
_____
_____
_____
_____
_____

" " QUOTE OF THE DAY
_____
_____
_____
_____

ONLY IN SEATTLE
_____
_____
_____
_____

SOMETHING I SAW TODAY

DAY
#____

DATE _____   RATING ☆☆☆☆☆

WEATHER ☀ ⛅ ☁ ☂ ❄

PLACES VISITED

_____
_____
_____
_____
_____
_____
_____
_____
_____

BEST EATS OF THE DAY

_____
_____
_____
_____
_____
_____
_____

QUOTE OF THE DAY

_____
_____
_____
_____

ONLY IN SEATTLE

_____
_____
_____
_____

SOMETHING I SAW TODAY

DAY

____

DATE _____   RATING ☆☆☆☆☆

WEATHER

PLACES VISITED
_____
_____
_____
_____
_____
_____
_____
_____
_____
_____

BEST EATS OF THE DAY
_____
_____
_____
_____
_____
_____
_____
_____
_____
_____

QUOTE OF THE DAY
_____
_____
_____
_____

ONLY IN SEATTLE
_____
_____
_____
_____

SOMETHING I SAW TODAY

_____

_____

_____

_____

_____

_____

_____

_____

_____

_____

_____

_____

_____

_____

_____

_____

_____

_____

LITERARY CITY

Did you know that Seattle has been designated by UNESCO (United Nations Educations, Scientific and Cultural Organization) as a City of Literature? So, grab a book, head to a local coffee shop, and sink into that new novel. You'll fit right in!

_____

_____

_____

_____

_____

_____

_____

OUTDOORSY SEATTLE

The search for an affordable, quality ice axe led outdoorsy folks Lloyd and Mary Anderson to create the wildly successful and popular co-op REI. In the Cascade neighborhood of Seattle (just next to South Lake Union) is REI's flagship store—a destination of its own including a forest setting, an outdoor firepit, a mini waterfall, a climbing wall, and much more.

_____

_____

_____

_____

_____

_____

_____

_____

_____

_____

_____

_____

_____

_____

_____

_____

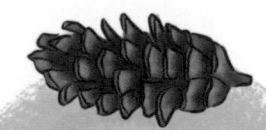

PARK TRAILS

By the sheer number of urban trails around Seattle, there's no hiding that Seattleites are big fans of the great outdoors. From circling Lake Union on a 6-mile loop to the ambitious almost-20-mile Burke-Gilman Trail, there are many options to get out and enjoy the scenery.

_____

_____

_____

_____

_____

_____

_____

_____

_____

_____

_____

_____

_____

_____

_____

_____

_____

_____

HOME TO TECH

Microsoft was just a small company when it moved to Bellevue (across Lake Washington from Seattle) in 1979. Lo and behold several decades later, the computer behemoth helped forge the way for many other high-tech companies to make Seattle one of the nation's fastest growing tech hubs.

_____

_____

_____

_____

_____

_____

_____

_____

_____

_____

_____

_____

_____

_____

_____

_____

_____

_____

_____

_____

_____

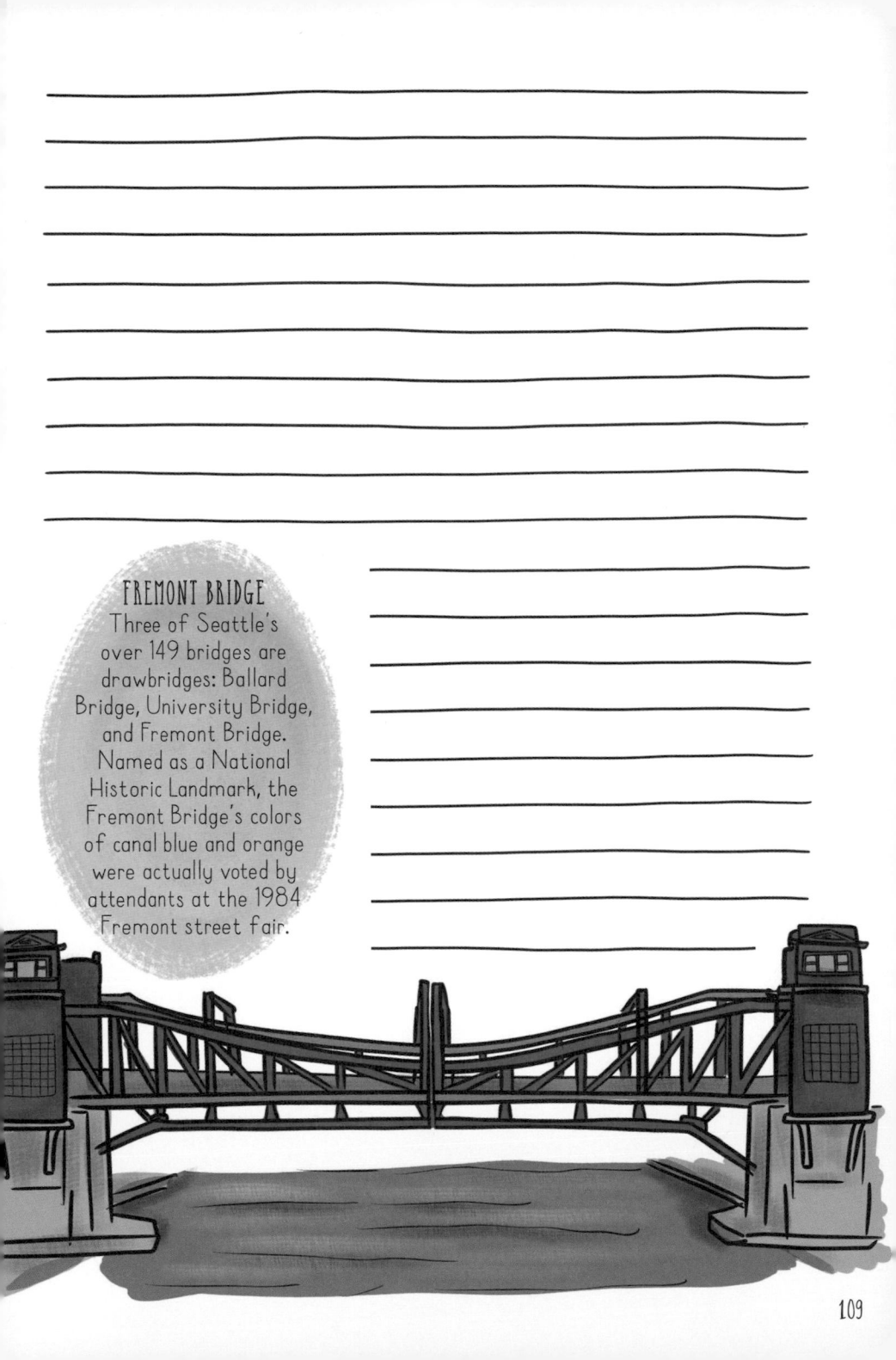

FREMONT BRIDGE
Three of Seattle's
over 149 bridges are
drawbridges: Ballard
Bridge, University Bridge,
and Fremont Bridge.
Named as a National
Historic Landmark, the
Fremont Bridge's colors
of canal blue and orange
were actually voted by
attendants at the 1984
Fremont street fair.

SUNNY SEATTLE

Hard to believe given all the rainy, drizzly days in their forecast, but it's been said that Seattleites buy more sunglasses per capita than any other major city in the US. Some locals claim the glare on wet roads is worse than the bright sun, while others report to losing their sunglasses often as they just don't wear them enough! Whether or not there is truth to the matter, be sure to pack a pair in case you do get some sunny days in Seattle.

DEDICATION

To my parents who have traveled to nearly every country in this world, thank you for continuing to teach me to embrace every experience and explore every corner!

Text and Illustrations © 2020 by Betsy Beier

Published by West Margin Press

ISBN: 9781513263007

LCCN: 2019057932

Proudly distributed by
Ingram Publisher Services

Printed in China
1 2 3 4 5

WEST MARGIN PRESS
WestMarginPress.com

WEST MARGIN PRESS
Publishing Director: Jennifer Newens
Marketing Manager: Angela Zbornik
Editor: Olivia Ngai
Design & Production: Rachel Lopez Metzger